The Lord's Prayer

The Seabury Press
815 Second Avenue
New York, N.Y. 10017

Copyright © 1975 by The Seabury Press, Inc.
Cover and interior design by Carl Weiss
Printed in the Unites States of America

Library of Congress Catalog Card Number : 75-13521
ISBN: 0-8164-2597-3

The Lord's Prayer

THE LORD'S PRAYER

Our Father, who art in heaven, hallowed be thy name, thy kingdom come, thy will be done, on earth as it is in heaven. Give us this day our daily bread. Forgive us our debts, as we forgive our debtors. Lead us not into temptation, but deliver us from evil. For thine is the kingdom and the power and the glory forever and ever. Amen.

THE
LORD'S
PRAYER

This is not a work of textual criticism. It is about the Lord's Prayer as a prayer. Nor is it an exercise in archaism, to discover precisely what it meant to those who first heard it and first prayed it. It is concerned with what praying it can mean to ourselves.

Catholics more often speak of it as the Our Father—in the Middle Ages it was the Paternoster to everybody. Others speak of it as the Lord's Prayer.

The title "Lord's Prayer" suggests that it was a prayer that Jesus himself prayed, but we tend to think of it rather as a pattern of prayer that he gave to his followers. Luke, we remember, says Christ gave it in answer to the request "Teach us how to pray," Matthew shows him as prefacing it with "Pray then like this."

Yet as we think our way through it, we shall find much of it is clearly his own prayer to his own Father. We may find ourselves wondering if any of it is not. However we may decide about this, there is gain in having asked ourselves at every one of its petitions whether Jesus might not have prayed it before us—whether he might not have given it to us, his brothers and sisters, because he himself had prayed it and found it good.

PRAYER

Prayer is conversation with God, speaking to him, listening to him. To believe in the God of Jesus Christ and never speak to him at all would surely be eccentric: for he is everywhere and everywhen; nowhere are we out of his presence, at every instant he is at the center of our being, more inward to us than we are to ourselves—which may sound like a shop-soiled spiritual cliché, but is literal truth. He may not be present to our awareness, we are always present to his.

In those who have fallen out of, or never had, the habit of prayer, there may be a willingness to admit that it would be more sensible to pray. But they feel embarrassed about it. What does one say to him? How break the silence?

For a beginning we should say whatever is in our minds, especially whatever bothers us. If complaining comes easiest, then complain—like St. Teresa, who said to God, "You treat your friends so badly, no wonder you have so few"; or like that odd French genius Léon Bloy, who said to God, "I wouldn't treat a mangey dog as you treat me." The Roman playwright Terence said, "Whatever concerns man concerns me." But long before Terence, God said it. Whatever concerns you or me concerns God.

So say it, whatever it is. Prayer is primarily getting it off our chests. And this same practice of just saying it is a beginning of return for those who, without wholly losing faith, find their certainty of God dim and their awareness vanished.

Any number of people have told me that they would feel fools getting down on their knees. The knees are not of the essence. No posture is. Just start saying. The knees may or may not come later. When that pleasing comedian, Phil Silvers, was interviewed about his meeting with Pope Pius XII, he was asked if he had knelt. He said of course. The interviewer said, ''But you are a Jew.'' Phil Silvers said, ''When you meet someone as holy as that, you find kneeling more comfortable.'' For myself, I never find kneeling comfortable. And it is not the point. Knees can be constraining and conversation with someone as close to us as God should have no constraint in it. We have no need to tidy up as for a distinguished visitor. Visitor is precisely what God is not. He is never not there.

Being what we are, we find our needs and our complaints bursting for utterance. But that could not make the whole of one's conversation with anybody. Conversation is not talking, but talking *with.* There must be an interest in the other party, an awareness of who it is one is talking with. At first our talking with God may be mainly about ourselves. But as it goes on awareness grows, intimacy grows, and full conversation is beginning. At the point where the sense of our own grievances begins to have a mingle of consciousness of the one we are complaining *to,* the Lord's Prayer may help us over the threshold.

Awareness of God means adoration—awareness of his holiness. This brings awareness of our own mediocrity—expressed in gratitude for all he has given us, sorrow for all our failures in his regard. Adoration, thanksgiving, contrition—these three are the foundation of the whole prayer relation.

But this relation allows for a fourth—petition, asking God for what we want, things spiritual, things material, for others, for

ourselves, I say "allows for," but it is stronger than that. If all these extra things mean a great deal to us, it would be abnormal not to tell God about them, it would be treating him as a stranger, which is one thing he does not want to be. Prayer, since it is conversation, means not only speaking but listening, the self quieting its clamor to allow God to make his own kind of communication. It is a wholly different kind—light given us to see, strength to act—wholly different, but no one who has any habit of prayer doubts its reality.

We begin with the silence which comes of having nothing to say. Then comes utterance, with growing depth of awareness. On the other side of utterance comes a new silence, having all the excellence of utterance, plus the excellence, special to itself, of absorption.

Of mystical contemplation I say nothing. It is a kind of fourth dimension of prayer, not clearly to be found in the Gospels, and not in the Lord's Prayer, which is our present topic: though one can imagine the Lord's Prayer rising into the prayer of mystical union. But it does not begin like that. The newcomer to prayer can find it first saying something *to* him, and then saying something *for* him.

THE
LORD'S
PRAYER

We find the Lord's Prayer in Matthew and in Luke. Matthew places it in the Sermon on the Mount, near the beginning of Christ's public ministry: Christ gives it as an example of saying what you have to say and not overloading your prayer with pointless repetition. Luke places it later, and shows it as Christ's answer to a disciple who had said, "Lord, teach us to pray, as John taught his disciples." The Luke version is shorter by two petitions—"Thy will be done on earth as in heaven" and "deliver us from evil." Each of these simply casts light on the one that precedes it—"Thy Kingdom come" and "lead us not into temptation." And Luke has a couple of minor differences which will be looked at as we come to them.

Both versions have the brevity which in Matthew is given as the reason why Christ gave us the Prayer. Matthew's has fifty-seven words, Luke's thirty-nine. It is surprising how much has been made of that eighteen-word difference. One writer thinks that Matthew has inserted "liturgical embellishments"—into eighteen words! Some find Matthew's version more eschatological, Luke's more here-and-now. The reader must make up his own mind.

More to the point is the question which was the original, or whether the original may not have been among the Logia of Christ

in the first—Aramaic—Matthew, which Papias mentions and we no longer have.

There seems to be general agreement among the learned that Luke's version came first (or is closest to the Aramaic Matthew's) —principally on the ground that his is shorter. But then Luke does shorten. He gives only four beatitudes as against Matthew's eight, and has them uttered "on a plain" not on a mountain. I think this last point of difference is the key to the solution. Christ was an outdoor speaker—I too for that matter. And men of this habit will say their most important things again and again, never twice exactly the same, varying according to the crowd's reactions. Christ must surely have given both the Beatitudes and Lord's Prayer, not twice but many times. Different Christian communities would have said the form of the prayer which came their way. Luke might have been using one such form, Matthew another, and so on. Had Mark and John recorded the prayer, they would probably have given it a little differently again. In favor of Matthew's placement is that Luke's is not wrought into the design of the chapter, it is simply dropped in there, and could as easily have been dropped into a dozen other chapters. Whereas, it fits not only the Sermon on the Mount but the events preceding the Sermon, quite miraculously. Every element in the prayer echoes, or gets light from, an element in the Sermon, or the Temptations in the Desert, or Christ's Baptism by John. It may be, of course, that it was Matthew who saw its place in the design, or perhaps created the design. My small vote is for Christ. In any event, I would urge anyone settling down to study the Prayer to read the Sermon first (Chapters 5 to 7), indeed to read Chapters 3 and 4 before the Sermon.

There is no record in the New Testament of the first Christians ever saying the Lord's Prayer. For that we must wait for the *Didache,* the Teaching of the Twelve, written some time before the end of the first century. It uses the Matthew version.

One thing the brevity of the Prayer reflects is the brevity of the whole Sermon. At an ordinary lecturing pace, it takes about twenty minutes. Considering that crowds had come from Galilee and Decapolis, Jerusalem, Judea and the country beyond Jordan—three days of journey for some of them—Jesus would hardly have sent them away with a twenty-minute talk. Clearly we are given the highlights, and splendid they are, but with a brilliance sometimes dimmed for us by the omissions.

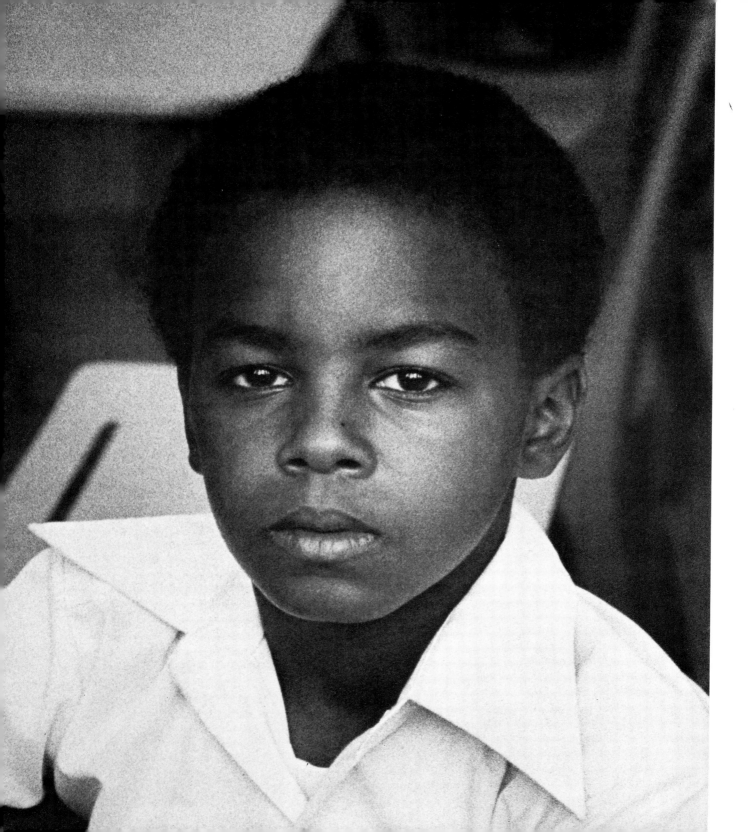

OUR

Christ has chosen to give mankind a pattern of prayer in terms not of I and my and me, but of we and our and us. I am asking God, for instance, to give the food life needs, not to *me*, but to *us*—i.e., me and all the other children of Our Father. So also with the forgiveness, without which sin may separate me *and them* from God. Luke omits "Our." He goes straight to "Father." But he has the other plurals. For this is a prayer of the family of God, not in the sense that it can be prayed only together with others, but that it must not, indeed cannot, be prayed save in awareness of those others.

OUR
FATHER

The first word we hear from Jesus is "Did you not know that I should be in my Father's house?" or maybe "On my Father's business?" The Greek merely has "my Father's" with no noun. His last words on the Cross were "Father, into thy hands I commend my spirit." In between the first word and the last we hear him talking of, or to, his Father again and again, almost continuously—some fifty times by a rough count. His own relation to the Father is special, unique: "No one knows the Son but the Father, no one knows the Father but the Son—*and him to whom the Son shall reveal him.*" Those last words are vital. Christ is not hugging his knowledge of the Father jealously to his own breast: he will communicate it to the limit of our power to receive it.

"I am the way," he says in answer to Thomas at the Last Supper—the way to what? To the Father. "No one comes to the Father but by me," so he completes the answer to Thomas. To bring us to the Father is his life's purpose.

Consider two statements he makes about his departure from this world, "I am ascending to my Father and your Father, to my God and your God." That is the first. The second: "I go to prepare a place for you. That where I am you may be."

And when at death we reach the goal, his words will be "Enter into the joy of my Father."

The Jews had a wonderful sense of God's Fatherhood, born of their release from slavery in Egypt and the long desert experience of God's closeness. "As a father pities his children, so the Lord pities them that fear him" (Psalm 103.13). There is even a comparison of God's care to a mother's, which cannot be matched in the New Testament—"Can a woman forget the child at her breast? . . . Even these may forget, yet will I not forget you" (Isaiah 49.15).

But it was primarily as father of Israel that they saw him, not of their individual selves. They had no habit of actually addressing God as their Father. Jesus does it continually. We remember "Father, forgive them, for they know not what they do." He even uses the affectionate "Abba," as he tells God of his agony in Gethsemane. And it is not simply out of the uniqueness of his own sonship that he speaks to God as Father. He urges his followers to do it. "Pray then like this: Our Father. . . ."

We are so used to it that we cannot imagine what it meant to his hearers. But it is worth noting that even his closest followers seem not to have found it easy. They could glory in the right Christ had won for them to say "Abba, Father," but there is no instance in the New Testament of any of them actually doing it. Paul comes close to it a couple of times, in his First Letter to the Thessalonians (3.11) and again in the Second (2.16): "Now may Our Lord Jesus Christ himself and God our Father, comfort your hearts."

Yes, the direct speech of son to Father took some getting used to. We of course are used to it, only too used to it perhaps. The shock has gone out of the words "Our Father," and with the shock much of the vitality. If we can speak the words with no sensation at all, barely noticing what we are saying, we should examine ourselves closely. The right to say them is one of the greatest gifts Christ won for us.

But what do the words mean? Or are they more than words? To compare God's care for us with a father's, or even a mother's, may be a useful figure of speech. But in what sense is he actually our Father? Christ answered surprisingly. "Call no man your father upon earth, for you have one Father who is in heaven" (Mt. 23.9). In other words, God's is the reality of Fatherhood; human fatherhood, spiritual or physical, is the figure of speech! The essence of fatherhood is the conveyance of life: God is the source of whatever life his surrogates convey to us. He is our Father, the rest are his deputies. So Paul can say to the Ephesians, "I bow my knee to my Father from whom all paternity in heaven or earth is named" (3.15).

But there is a deeper order of life. We must be born again, says Christ, enter into a second life, a second sonship therefore, indwelt by God as Christ himself is: a life we enter by water and the Holy Spirit—receiving Christ, believing in his name, we become at this new level children of God—"born, not of blood or of the will of the flesh, or of the will of man, but of God" (John 1.13). Of this life Christ makes no mention in the Lord's Prayer. He had not yet revealed it.

A father is not only the source of existence. If that were all, once we have come into existence his fatherly function would be over. The relation is for life. But what sort of relation? The Old Testament father is warned against spoiling the child—he must use the rod lavishly. The typical Jewish father may not have been as tough as that sounds. But there must have been some reason for St. Paul's twice urging parents not to stir their children to resentment.

And among ourselves there is the father that mothers threaten naughty small boys with. In any event that is not the fatherhood Our Lord sees in God. He shows that Father as knowing, hearing, listening, caring, loving, giving himself: God clothes the grasses of

[34]

the field: no sparrow falls without God's seeing. He can withdraw himself, but only in the face of man's refusal. There is no refusal in God, only in man. The picture that stays in the mind is of the father going out to meet the Prodigal Son.

WHO
ART
IN
HEAVEN

Just as Luke has not "Our" before the word Father, he has not "Who are in heaven" after it. "In heaven" is not there for nothing, inserted we might think to make the opening words more solemn, more liturgical. It is a reminder that God is not within the limits of this world, which absorbs us so totally, submerges us, all but drowns us. God is everywhere, of course, which means that we can pray to him anywhere, as in the kindly epitaph someone wrote over the grave of a man thrown from his horse—

> *Between the stirrup and the ground*
> *Mercy I sought, mercy I found.*

But Scripture constantly links the word heaven with the word God, and not only in the Old Testament where we might suspect a mental reaching back to the sky gods of the great paganisms. Our Lord himself loves to make the connection. A score of times in

Matthew's Gospel we find him using the phrases "Father in heaven" or "Heavenly Father."

The word "heaven" is indeed used in Scripture for the sky, but with more and more awareness that with all its immensity, the sky is still too small for him.

"Heaven and the heaven of heavens cannot contain thee, how much less this house I have built." Whatever that meant to Solomon, we know that it is not a matter of largeness, with God overlapping on every side the universe he made of nothing!

God's omnipresence, ubiquity, everywhereness, does not mean God thinly spread over all that is, so that there is no part of the universe which does not get some of him—the idea which puzzled Augustine as he was thinking his way to the Faith. God is not in space. Space is the arrangement matter makes to spread its parts in: but God is a spirit, with all that he is and all that he does in one single act of being, with no parts to spread! "God is everywhere" means that nothing is out of reach of his knowledge and love and power. God is, is present, where he acts—wherever his power and knowledge and love reach, that is everywhere.

For Our Lord, heaven is God being wholly himself, living his own life with the Son and the Spirit, seen face to face by the angels, to be seen face to face and rejoiced in by all who have not refused him.

A moment ago I wondered what concept Solomon may have had of God's omnipresence. But we might do worse in our own churches than pray as he did about the Temple (I Kings 8.27): "Have regard to the prayer of thy servant . . . that thy eyes may be open night and day towards this house . . . that thou mayst hearken to the prayer which thy servant offers towards this place and hear thou in heaven thy dwelling place; and when thou hearest forgive.''

HALLOWED
BE
THY
NAME

We have here two words "hallowed" and "name"—out of which most of the life has drained. Neither word stirs in us the resonances that they stirred in the Jews who heard Jesus say them. It would be gain for us to feel some of those resonances. Hallowed is a word from the adjective holy; we hallow, feel as sacred, not only God but whatever we see as especially God's or used in his service. In the Old Testament, among things hallowed, we find priests, the king, the sabbath, the first-born in Israel, the bread of the Presence, the Temple. Moses is told (Exodus 3.5): "Take off your shoes, for the place on which you are standing is holy ground."

We today are still prepared to think of God as holy, but we seem to have little sense of the sacredness of things that are especially related to God. This reacts on our awareness of God himself —seeing the sacredness of these lesser things would have helped to keep the nerve alive which can react to his supreme sacredness. We cannot read the Old Testament without feeling almost bodily the Jewish awareness of God's majesty—awe, reverential fear. We ourselves can still feel a sudden catching of the breath at poetry or scenery or a woman's beauty or human heroism or self-sacrifice. Do we ever feel anything like this about God himself?

Our human organism, of course, could not stay permanently at the level of adoration God can at moments lift us to, if he is continually real to us. But never to have felt the lift of adoration at all means a life pulse of religion that has not throbbed in us. Religion would be a colorless affair if God became little more than a name prayed to dutifully, still worse prayed to as a last straw, not very hopefully.

When, in the pattern of prayer he was giving them, Our Lord came to "Hallowed be thy name," his hearers would have known it as one they had heard before. In Leviticus we find God saying, "You shall not profane my holy name, but I will be hallowed among the people of Israel" (22.23). When Pope John said of the Christian churches not in communion with himself: "They bear the name of Christ on their forehead," I for one did not remember a phrase of Exodus (28.36): "You shall make a plate of pure gold and engrave on it Holy to the Lord. . . . It shall be on Aaron's forehead."

In Scripture and in Jewish speech generally, "Name" was charged with a richness of significance which it has not on our lips. For us a name is hardly more than a label, a convenience of speech to indicate which individual we are talking about. A number would get the same result as efficiently. A man in love can go beyond this, feeling a sort of ecstasy in saying a woman's name. Men have been known to feel that way about God: yet not necessarily about his name.

But for Scripture a name was not a label, a convenience; the name was the very reality of the thing, the reality as uttered, all the more real for the utterance. "Hallowed be thy name" means holy to us be God himself, as our mind unites with him in uttering him. There should be no question of saying God's name without our minds united to his, saying God's name with our minds on something else, least of all in support of falsehood. Indeed, his own personal name Yahweh, which is himself as the plenitude and source of existence, was so sacred that it was scarcely to be uttered with the lips at all, and not even written in full—only the consonants YHWH.

Ritual actions, ritual silences, all helped to keep alive in them the sense of God's majesty, of his infinite Otherness yet infinite closeness.

We have so largely opted against rituals. The function they once performed of keeping a fine edge on men's awareness of God they do not perform for us. We must find some other way to keep our awareness of God unblunted. To preserve the sacredness of Yahweh they used special ways of addressing God without saying his all-holy name. Most fascinatingly they referred to him as the Name! Leviticus tells of a man stoned to his death for "blaspheming the Name." *We* should not do that, of course. But does hearing God blasphemed stir us to any sort of anguish for the state of the soul out of which the blasphemy came?

It goes with hallowing God's *name,* that we should give our whole mind to God's *self.* We should study his words and his works to grow in our knowledge of him: each new thing learned about him is a new reason for loving him.

The name is not enough. Rituals can become a routine—words and actions expressing nothing in the mind or will, yet leaving one soothed in the consciousness of duty to God rightly rendered.

An extreme instance Christ himself gives—men who were startled to hear him say to them, "I never knew you, depart from me, you evildoers." They protested that they had prophesied in his name, cast out devils in his name, worked many miracles in his name. His answer is appallingly final: "Not everyone who says to me 'Lord, Lord' shall enter the kingdom of heaven, but he who does the will of my Father."

At the other extreme is the student of theology who can fall so deeply in love with the formulas into which theology has cast its findings that these can become an end in themselves, an obsession.

Theology can wrap God in a cloud—for them and their pupils—so that they see only the cloud, and a very cloudy cloud it can be. Philosophy is the handmaid of theology but theology is the handmaid of living awareness.

So we try to meet God in our minds, but must constantly return to the Scriptures and the Eucharist for two special ways of contact with his reality. We should, for instance, refresh our understanding of the Lord's Prayer by a careful rereading of the Sermon on the Mount in which Matthew has enshrined it. Every key word of the Prayer receives its comment in the Sermon.

THY
KINGDOM
COME

John the Baptist had been preaching a baptism of repentance for the forgiveness of sins, crying out that the Kingdom of God was at hand. When he was arrested by Herod Antipas, Christ Our Lord took up where John had left off. He went into Galilee and began his preaching of the same warning—''The time is fulfilled, the Kingdom of God is at hand, repent,'' adding the new element ''Believe in the Gospel,'' that is the good news. Clearly the coming of the Kingdom was of vital importance to both of them.

The Greek word here suggests ''kingship,'' rather than ''kingdom.'' Neither is a word of much living vigor in our world. With the deposing and humiliating of Ethiopia's king, Haile Selassie, who boasted the Queen of Sheba as ancestress a hundred generations back, the only recent king whose name springs to mind is Feisal of Saudi Arabia. He glories in an ancestress a thousand years further back still, Hagar, driven into the desert with her (and Abraham's) son Ishmael by Isaac's mother, Sara. One lists these improbabilities as a reminder how very much alive kingship was in the world out of which the Israel of Jesus came. In that Israel it still had vitality. Jesus' hearers were expecting a restoration of David's kingdom, with Israel given a world dominance which even David had not known. When on the lips of the new miracle worker they heard the words ''thy kingdom come'' many of them must have felt that David's moment was upon them.

In the Old Testament, indeed, there is one solitary mention of David's Kingdom as the Kingdom of Yahweh (1 Chron. 28.5). But it was not of that kind of kingdom that Jesus and the Baptist talked— they placed too much emphasis on repentance and sins to be forgiven, and there was a chilling phrase of John's about putting the axe to the root of the tree which gave no comfort to the Establishment. Very sensibly, it must have felt, it killed them both.

As it turned out, it was for preaching the Kingdom that Christ was slain. Without that his enemies could not have forced the Roman Procurator to have him crucified. As the first question Pontius Pilate asked him, all four Gospels have: ''Are you the King of the Jews?'' And kingship runs through the whole trial.

Since they had thrown off the yoke of their own kings five hundred years before, kingship remained a scar in the Roman psyche needing only to be scratched to bleed. Apart from that, their instinct for government told them that a rebellion in one of their provinces could grow most vigorously round a ''king''; at any hint of a king a nerve throbbed in them. We know that at one time they decided to seek out descendants of King David and have them slain—only to discover that they had sunk to such a point of poverty and no esteem that they were not worth killing: one of them we remember was a village carpenter. Christ's enemies knew what line to take with Pilate.

But the Roman official saw quickly that Christ was no threat—no threat anyhow that he could recognize. John's account in his 18th and 19th chapters of what passed between them is as fascinating as anything in all Scripture. To the question as to his own kingship the prisoner answered, ''My kingship is not of this world. . . . For this I was born, and for this I have come into the world, to bear witness to the truth. Everyone that is of the truth hears my voice.'' That was enough for Pilate. His answer was equivalent to ''Pouf, is that all?''

But the king motif sounded again and again. The soldiers put a purple robe on him and a crown of thorns and hailed him as king.

Pilate wished to release him—whether from an official dislike of injustice when it did not profit him personally, or from a personal dislike of being bullied by the Jewish leaders whom he hated. But the leaders played their trump card—"If you release him you are not Caesar's friend. Whoever makes himself a king sets himself against Caesar." Pilate was beaten. But he made two more efforts. "He said, 'Here is your king.' And again, 'Shall I crucify your king?' " And the chief priests—Sadducees, not Pharisees—shouted out their apostasy—"We have no king but Caesar."

On Christ's cross Pilate had a writing put: "Jesus of Nazareth, the King of the Jews." As Jesus hung there dying, he was taunted, "Christ, King of Israel, come down from the cross." And one of the thieves crucified with him said "Remember me when you come into your kingdom."

What did Christ mean by the Kingdom? As his followers reported him, we find references to an everlasting kingdom which might have reminded them of the one Daniel (Chapter 4) had said God was preparing for the saints; references are more frequent to a kingdom on the point of appearing here below. It is called the Kingdom of God, it is called Kingdom of Heaven (especially in Matthew's Gospel, written for Jewish Christians and mindful of their reverent shrinking from using the name God).

While for citizenship in the Kingdom there must be *metanoia*— a change of mind and heart—it is not to be an invisible kingdom existent only in the minds and hearts of those who love God and their fellow men. That was not what Jesus meant when he told Pilate his kingship was not of this world. Its origin was in the will of God, but it was to have a framework here upon earth. For he speaks of entry into it by rebirth of water and the Holy Spirit, of publicans and harlots granted entry and priests refused. Most notably he speaks of "the Keys of the Kingdom of heaven"—seeing it as a walled city, at war with Hell, seen also as a walled city with its gates.

But the structure was not the main point, nor the officials. The officials, Christ said, were to serve. The structure was to protect the life of the Kingdom.

One mysterious thing he said, along with the promise that the Kingdom was near at hand—"The Kingdom of God is in the midst of you" (Luke 17.21). It seems that it was his own presence among them that he had in mind. The Kingdom is himself, and the Church at one with him. Of this Kingdom the Sermon on the Mount gives us the charter. And the life principle is to do the will of God. Which looks forward to the next petition in the pattern of prayer he has given us.

Pilate saw that the Kingdom Christ preached called for no intervention from him. Christ's enemies knew it too, they had their own reasons for wanting him dead, on any terms. But what, we wonder, did they think he meant by the Kingdom? We can hardly blame them if they did not know. His own chosen followers were slow to grasp it.

One of the most surprising incidents in his life on earth came when he was about to leave it. Between his rising from the dead and his ascension into heaven, Acts tells us he appeared to the Apostles during forty days, "speaking of the Kingdom of God." And the last question they asked him—"Lord, will you at this time restore the Kingdom to Israel?"

Slowly the structure emerged, and a time came when to many the structure seemed all-important. But the life of the Kingdom was, as we have seen, what the Kingdom existed for, indeed what the King-

dom consisted in. Paul the Apostle, who was not there when Christ ascended, was to say it for all of them (Romans 14.17): "The Kingdom of God means righteousness and peace and joy in the Holy Spirit."

THY
WILL
BE
DONE

This is one of the two petitions not in Luke's version of the prayer. Like the other omitted petition, this one casts light on the one before it. It is the essence of the meaning of "Thy Kingdom come," giving it precision. The Kingdom exists wherever God's will is done—I had almost said wherever the doing of God's will is seriously attempted. In one sense it is merely a clarifying. But it is so richly clarifying. If it was an afterthought, it was an inspiration.

This emphasis on God's will is not a servile crouching before a despot. Even apart from our habit of clutching at what we want and evading what costs us too much, our own will is a poor guide. There is so much that we don't know, so much that we know wrong. What the future holds for us we cannot know, what the present plainly holds for us, we are bad at seeing. God has total vision of reality, choosing our own will against his is opting for the unreal. It is the plain truth that he knows us better than we know ourselves, that he cares more for our happiness than we care ourselves. Dante has it exactly right—"In his will is our peace."

We have raised the question how far Our Lord himself prayed the Lord's Prayer. Upon this petition we are left in no doubt. In Gethsemane he prayed it for himself, in agony. He had begged: "If it be possible let this cup pass from me." A second time he prayed: "My Father, if this cannot pass unless I drink it, thy will be done" (Mt.26.42).

At no point do we feel Christ's brotherhood closer or clearer. We have all said it, not at the extremity of pressure which wrung the cry from him, but under pressure which seemed fierce enough to ourselves. Nor do we all attain the serenity of acceptance in which he could say, "Shall I not drink the cup which the Father has given me?"

"Thy will be done," with its hardly avoidable extension "Thy will, not mine," is the key to the Lord's Prayer as it was to the Lord's whole life. It is the point of maturity for every one of us, as it was for him.

The writer of Hebrews—read all of Chapter 5—must have had Gethsemane vividly in his mind when he wrote "Though he was Son, he learnt obedience by the things he suffered." That is surprising enough. This Jesus whose Father's name was so continually on his lips, whose food was to do his Father's will, what had he to learn about obedience? What was to be thought about obedience, he had not to learn. But there are things to be learned about obedience by obeying—unsayable, enriching things.

The continuation in Hebrews is even more surprising: "being made perfect, he became the means of salvation to those who obey him." "Being made perfect" does not mean there had been imperfection in him and it was in him no longer. It means that he had achieved a new kind of perfection, his humanity was now totally adequate to the divine personality. His very being was greater for the obedience which lived on through the suffering. The Christ who went to death saying "Father, into thy hands I commend my spirit," was a greater human being (if I may say the unsayable) than the Christ who could say "I am the Resurrection and the Life" as he brought Lazarus back from the dead.

That is what obedience did for him.

ON
EARTH
AS
IT
IS IN
HEAVEN

This phrase concludes the first part of the Prayer and applies to all three of its petitions. In heaven, Christ is saying, God's name is hallowed perfectly, God's kingship is accepted perfectly, God's will is done perfectly—by the angels, I take it, who as he was to say, "see the face of my heavenly Father continually" (Mt. 18.10). We must pray that they may be served perfectly here on earth too.

He does not see earth and heaven as polar opposites, but related as means to end, way to goal, pilgrimage to shrine. Life, too, is not just a second best, a kind of slumming, to be lived through somehow, with perfection postponed till after death. We must aim at perfection here. Before reaching the Lord's Prayer he had told them in the Sermon "You must be perfect as your heavenly Father

is perfect.'' He was not telling them to be infinite or absolute, but to lack no goodness that ought to be present in the kind of creature man is.

He does not suggest that perfection is easy: he told the rich young man (Mt. 19.21) that perfection for him would mean selling all he had and giving the proceeds to the poor. The young man thought this too high a price to pay for perfection. Most of us set a limit beyond which we will not readily force ourselves to go. But every time we say the Lord's Prayer we are asking God to help us towards perfection, even if its full price we still shrink from paying. Doing his will is the only rule. As Augustine says grimly: To be virtuous we have only to will it. Only.

ASKING
GOD
FOR
THINGS

So far the Lord's Prayer concerns itself with our relationship to God, our sonship, our adoration, our obedience, the union of our will with his. None of these is possible to us without the life and light God gives us, and for these we pray: but his kingdom will come only as we respond to them.

Of the elements we have seen as prayer's foundation—adoration, thanksgiving, contrition—we have been uttering the first; the third, contrition, is to come as we pray for forgiveness; the second, thanksgiving, does not come into the Prayer at all. We may feel this strange, for thanksgiving seemed to be part of the air Christ breathed. Indeed we feel it in the very air of this prayer in which it is not mentioned. Basic to all we ask God for is gratitude to a God who has told us to ask him.

In any event sonship, adoration, obedience are the context *in* which, the relation between ourselves and God *from* which, we pray. We do not explicitly remind ourselves of them every time we say the Our Father, or any other prayer. They should have become part of the self which says the prayer, part also of the self which rises into the silence that lies on the other side of utterance.

All the same, it's good to go over them from time to time, above all when we are asking God for things. This, for the rest of its brief length, the Our Father guides us in doing.

The first two things we ask for are daily bread and forgiveness of our sins. Daily bread is the minimum for our bodily need, forgiveness the minimum for our spiritual.

In the prayer for bread we are brought face to face with the troubling question of the things we pray for and do not get. Thousands who have asked the Father for their daily bread have died of starvation. Paul says "We have the mind of Christ," the *nous,* the knowing power, the element in him by which he saw things as they are. We cannot hope to see all that he saw. But we must do all that lies in us to find out what he was actually saying.

In the Sermon, for instance, he says: "Ask and you shall receive." At the Last Supper he says "Ask the Father anything in my name and he will give it to you." If he meant "anything" literally, the universe would cease to be a universe and would become first a carnival and then a chaos—with every believer asking whatever might strike him as desirable. He could have meant it only of what is necessary for our eternal well-being, which, we must remember, was a reality always vividly present to him, the reason why he had to come.

St. Paul could say "The sufferings of this present time are not worth comparing with the glory that is to be revealed to us" (Romans 8.18). If I had said that, one might ask "What do you know about sufferings?" But it was Paul, and we have his answer to the question: "Five times I have received at the hands of the Jews the forty lashes less one, three times beaten with rods, once stoned, three times shipwrecked, a night and a day adrift on the sea, in danger from robbers, from my own people, from Gentiles, from false brethren, in danger in the city, in the wilderness, at sea." (2 Corinthians 11:23-4).

None of this does Our Lord bring into the Lord's Prayer. What he gives is the reminder that in joy or in agony, prayer granted or not granted, we are in the hands of our heavenly Father.

Two instances of things asked for and not given spring to mind. The most stunning instance is, of course, Christ's own prayer in Gethsemane. But Paul also has to tell of a refusal sufficiently surprising. He is afflicted by a sting in the flesh: he gives no detail, but of its urgency he leaves us in no doubt: he calls it "an angel of Satan which buffets me." Three times, he tells us, he begs God to free him from it. He is not freed. God says "My grace is sufficient for you."

It is no chance that the last words we say before the asking begins are "Thy will be done." Unless "Yet not my will but yours" is part of our asking, we are not praying at all.

The whole reason for asking God is the certainty that he can do things that we can't. Why? Because he has not only all power but all knowledge and all love. Therefore it is half-witted to try to force on him the choice made by our own half-knowledge and rather

tattered love. What we should include in every request is a prayer for grace not to resent its non-granting. "Non-granting" is a phrase that might mislead. The Spanish proverb quoted at the beginning of *The Satin Slipper* by Paul Claudel says it neatly—"God writes straight with crooked lines." Most of us have had the experience of being refused the thing we asked and getting a better. And there are strange "answers." Christ spent all one night in prayer to God, then chose the Twelve. Including Judas.

There is, of course, the probability that one might pray with practically no awareness of God at all, simply on the ground that prayer can do no harm, anything is worth trying—as an unbeliever might have a St. Christopher medal on his car.

GIVE
US
THIS
DAY
OUR
DAILY
BREAD

There is an immediate problem about "daily." The Greek word *epiousion,* used by both Matthew and Luke, is found only in the Lord's Prayer, so that we cannot be sure what it means. I have come across mention of a papyrus in which it is found, but if it exists it throws no light. There is a verbal difference about "this day" used by Matthew: Luke has "day by day." Either way, we are asking for bread sufficient for a day. In the Sermon Jesus says the same about troubles—today's are what we should bother about, "do not be anxious about tomorrow's, tomorrow will have its own anxieties."

The point is that concentrating on our own material well-being beyond the immediate need has two ill effects: (a) it distracts us from more fully human activities—thinking, studying, praying, helping the needy; (b) it can grow into an obsession, the occupational hazard of the rich. From the camel and the needle's eye to the rich fool who looked forward to taking his ease, eating, drinking, being merry, the sin Christ returns to most is preoccupation with wealth.

FORGIVE US OUR DEBTS

Strange that the word "trespasses" should have shouldered out "debts" in the Prayer as said by Catholics of the English tongue. Not that it is a bad word in the context, but it is a word that has died, living on only in the meaning of walking on someone else's property. The Latin word used in the Vulgate and in the Church's liturgy is *debita.* The Greek word used by Matthew is *opheilemata,* which also means debts—primarily debts of money, but having the wider sense of any failure to meet one's obligations.

What are our obligations to God? The Prayer has already listed them. We must hallow his Name, we must live by the laws of his Kingdom, we must do his Will. We fall short of our obligations most obviously by our sins, and that is the word Luke uses here. But even with no stateable sin committed, no stateable duty sinfully omitted, can we feel that we have given God all that we should of adoration, that we have brought our will totally into harmony with his?

This is a matter in which the saints have a greater sensitivity. We read of a saint in an agony of contrition for what we should regard as no sin at all. We feel he is overdoing it. We should be only too pleased if we had so little to be contrite for. It is rather like a violinist in a state of anguish over a performance which has seemed to me quite wonderfully good. But he is comparing himself not with me but with Menuhin. The saint is comparing himself not with me but with Christ.

Did Christ ever pray this prayer himself? He could say in all confidence, "Who will convict me of sin?" But did he ever feel he might have done his Father's will more perfectly, or loved his Father more? It is no very fervent lover who thinks he has loved enough.

He warned his followers: "When you have done all that is

commanded you, say, 'We are unprofitable servants, we have done only what was our duty.' '' He has not told us if he ever felt like that about his own service of God. If he did, it must have been comforting to hear the Voice from heaven—''This is my beloved Son, in whom I am well pleased.''

But for the mass of people no such delicate question arises. Our sins stare us in the face. From now to the end of the Lord's Prayer sin is the topic—its commission, the temptation to it, its avoidance, its forgiveness. By a mere count of words half the Prayer is concerned with sin. We cannot take Jesus seriously if we take sin lightly. He was called Jesus, which means Savior, said the angel, because he was to save his people from their sins. His preaching of the Kingdom began with the word ''Repent.'' There is nothing to compare in urgency with his will to save sinners. When he said to the paralyzed man, ''Your sins are forgiven,'' the man (and the bearers who had lowered him through the roof) must have felt sick with disappointment: he had come hoping for a cure of his paralysis. When Jesus said, ''Take up your bed and walk,'' the man surely felt all-paradisal. But Jesus had not been just tantalizing him with the smaller gift before meeting his hope and granting the greater: for Jesus the forgiveness was greater, beyond all comparison. I have said we cannot take Jesus seriously if we take sin lightly: we cannot take ourselves seriously if our sins concern us less than they concerned him. It is part of our drawing closer to him that we should see sin as he saw it, which includes seeing why it filled him with such horror.

Why was the healing of man's sinfulness of such urgency to Jesus? Primarily because it is the thrust of our own will against God's: God's will is the order of reality, sin breaks the order, adulterates reality with falsity; great sins adulterate it greatly, small sins in their small proportion. The effect of my sins on the totality of the real may be slight. Their effect upon the section of reality which is myself can be catastrophic. They mutilate or at least mar the image and likeness of God in which I and all men are made and in which my very identity and theirs consists. Every sin diminishes the life in us; to adapt a French phrase, *Pécher c'est mourir un peu* —every sin is a small dying. Serious sin is suicidal.

Yet in the run of life we find it hard to feel it so: we can get used to our own particular sin: we

> *Compound for sins we are inclined to*
> *By damning those we have no mind to.*

Other people's sins, we feel, are inexcusable, sheerly perverse, but ours—

The practice we call Examination of Conscience—gazing steadily, last thing at night, at what we have done during the day—can help us to see ourselves straight. In the quiet of the night the clamor of self-interest can sound like what it is, the craving for self-assertion can look its proper worst. The clutching, evading self is the cross we have to bear: all hope lies in our feeling it as a cross.

It is clear, then, that if we wish to live mentally in the real world, we must measure sins not by our own evaluation but by Christ's. There are sins, says Our Lord, that defile a man, that is, they make him dirty. In the seventh chapter of Mark he provides a list of them—not covering every imaginable or conceivable sin, but based on the Ten Commandments and quite sufficient for most of us. If few commit them all, there must be fewer still who commit none of them—evil thoughts, fornication, theft, murder, adultery, coveting, malice, deceit, licentiousness, envy, slander, pride, foolishness!

We may glance at two words in the list, malice and foolishness. Malice first. There is a distinction between pleasure in the evil action and pleasure in its evilness. "Evil be thou my good"—Milton has Satan say that, Satan who has already said "Myself am hell." I felt a whiff of this in a young man who prefers to seduce Catholic girls, because they think it's a sin.

Foolishness seems a mild ending to so formidable a list of sins. But it is an ingredient of every one of them. For each is a choice of one's own will against God's will. But since God made us, as he made all things, of nothing, only his will holds us in existence: if he withdrew his will, we should cease to exist. Every believer knows this. To think we can gain anything by action contrary to the will which alone holds us in being is sheer idiocy. Which does not, unfortunately, keep us from sinning, but does ensure that we shall feel fools while doing it.

It can happen that the pleasure the sin seems to promise is so great that a man can decide to grab the pleasure and damn the consequences. It is something at least to know what the consequences can be. Our Lord leaves us in no doubt. He says of a man who looks lustfully at a woman that he has committed adultery in his heart. And he adds the grim comment: If your eye leads you into sin (he adds hand and foot for good measure), it would be better to lose it, pluck it from you and throw it away (hand and foot too). Better to enter eternal life with body mutilated than to die whole in body and be cast into hell.

AS
WE
FORGIVE
OUR
DEBTORS

The Greek of Matthew reads "*as* we have forgiven our debtors," Luke has "*for* we have forgiven our debtors."

We have not yet heard Christ state the two commandments—love God, love your neighbor—on which all the others depend, their life principle. But already in the Sermon he has said one of the most improbable things to come from man's lips—"Love your enemies, do good to them that hate you."

All that he has to say of human conduct concerns ways either of fulfilling the two commands of love or of refusing them. The love we owe our fellow-men—thus also he makes it possible to bring under one of two headings, giving and forgiving. Any failure in either is a failure in love; unrepented, each is a failure in life, leading to eternal loss.

The refusal to give—food and drink to the hungry and thirsty, clothing and shelter to men stripped and homeless—means damnation. But he is just as harsh on refusal to forgive. One of his most terrible parables is of the servant who received mercy and showed none (Matthew 18). His master had forgiven him a very large sum he owed: he then had a fellow servant imprisoned who owed him a very small sum. Hearing of this, the master cancelled the first forgiveness and the merciless one was cast into prison with small probability that he would ever come out. The parable uses the same Greek words for "debt" and "forgive" as the Lord's Prayer uses.

It is not that one forgiveness balances the other and sets the accounts straight—balances the cosmic books, so to speak—but that refusal to forgive is a failure of love, an open sore, a suppuration in the self.

I think the best-known sentence in the Sermon on the Mount is the one we call the Golden Rule—do unto others as you would have them do to you. In the light of the condition attached to our own forgiveness in the Lord's Prayer, we can add a corollary—do unto others as we would have God do to us. We ask him to forgive us, and we must forgive. We have just asked him to give us our daily bread—we must help to feed the hungry. We are about to ask him to lead us not into temptation, and to deliver us from evil—we must be careful not to lead others into temptation, still less tempt them, and we must regard aid to others threatened by physical or moral evil as a first call upon ourselves.

It all goes with the use of the first person plural—we, our, us—instead of the first person singular. The first person singular is the last person we shall ever manage to bring under control—under the first person singular's control, that is!

LOOKING
TOWARDS
THE
WORLD'S
END

We have still two petitions of the Lord's Prayer to discuss—"Lead us not into temptation" and "Deliver us from evil." I have seen it argued that the wording of the Greek makes it grammatically necessary to see the *temptation* as a single great happening. And there are scholars who think that both the *temptation* into which we pray not be led, and the *evil* from which we pray to be delivered, refer to the great crisis which will herald the end of the world.

In the 24th chapter of Matthew we have Our Lord's description of how calamitous the last onslaught will be—"Many will fall away, and betray one another and hate one another. . . . Most men's love will grow cold. But he who endures to the end will be saved. . . . There will be great tribulation such as has not been from the beginning of the world until now. . . . And if those days had not been shortened, no human being would be saved; but for the sake of the elect those days will be shortened."

My own feeling is that the four final petitions like the first three are both eschatological and actual. They look ahead to the *eschata*, the last things: but they consider what must happen *meanwhile* if these are to be brought to final accomplishment. That there will be a vast temptation at the end makes it all the more necessary that mankind should learn to cope with the lesser (but still fierce) temptations of every day. "On earth as it is in heaven" refers not only to "thy will be done" but also to "hallowed be thy name" and "thy kingdom come." Similarly "daily" refers not only to bread, but to daily debts, daily temptations, daily evil. All three of these we have to cope with. They are horribly daily.

LEAD
US
NOT
INTO
TEMPTATION

As the phrase stands, it is bothering. It seems to imply two things—(1) for some reason it is our heavenly Father's habit to lead us into situations in which we are likely to sin against him and lose our souls; (2) but if we beg him not to, he won't—which would be fantastic, of course.

When I was young I solved the problem to my own satisfaction in two ways which now make me smile. Before I had so much as dipped my toes into Greek I read the petition as, "Lead us not-into temptation," in other words "away from" temptation. When I did dip my toes into Greek (I never dipped much more) I got the general feeling that the word order did not matter, that the negative word at the beginning of the sentence could be read as negating not the verb "lead" but the preposition "into": so I was back with "not-into," away-from.

I smile now. And of course it was largely unnecessary. I had not grasped that the key to the sentence lay in the word "temptation," which has a different emphasis in Scripture. With us it always conveys the idea of our being attracted—the tempter merely has to meet us half way. But in Scripture the meaning is almost always "test"—whether or not there is any movement towards yielding in the person "tempted."

The phrase as Christ used it in the Lord's Prayer is still puzzling because it crowds a great deal into five words. But it reads like an appeal to God so to guide our steps that we may not be tempted beyond our strength. That, anyhow, is how Paul read it (I Corinthians 10.12).

If the Lord's Prayer was uttered, as Matthew has it, in the course of the Sermon on the Mount, then Jesus had special cause to know what being led into temptation can mean—he had just come from the three testings by the devil.

Matthew tells us that, immediately after the voice had said "This is my beloved Son in whom I am well pleased," Jesus had been led by the Spirit into the desert *in order to be tempted* by the devil. Mark has a stronger word than "led"—the Spirit *drove* him into the desert, *ekballei,* almost hurled. (The verb is used for divorcing a wife, throwing her out of the house!) We cannot, I think, get the force of "Lead us not into temptation" or of "Deliver us from evil" unless we remember Christ's desert experience with the evil one. Whether or not it happened immediately before he taught the Lord's Prayer, it must always have been vividly present to him. That particular confrontation, however we understand it, belonged with his function as redeemer of the human race. But in the memory of it, he could not want us to have our resolution tested so searchingly.

The Epistle to the Hebrews says it clearly: "We have not a high priest who is unable to sympathise with our weaknesses but one who in every respect has been tempted—i.e., tested—as we are, yet without sin" (4.15). His testings must have brought his compassion to its perfection, as his suffering brought his obedience.

For notice, tested we *must* be. At the beginning of the Epistle of Christ's cousin James we find something that might strike us as wholly incredible, almost a contradiction of "Lead us not into temptation." "Count it all joy when you meet various trials"—that same Greek word, *peirasmon,* for temptation in the Lord's Prayer and for the temptations in the desert. James goes on: "For you know that the testing of your faith produces steadfastness. . . . Blessed is the man who endures trials (still *peirasmon*), for when he has stood the test, he will receive the crown of life God has promised to those who love him.''

Christ himself, as we see, had to be tested (a) for our sakes—because he himself had been tempted he is able to help those who are tempted; (b) for his own sake—he learned obedience and was made perfect, as Hebrews tells us. Look again at ''Lead us not'' in the meaning of ''guide us away from.'' There can indeed be testings that God wants us to undergo for our own strengthening, and in these we can but pray that he will help us not to fail.

But most of the situations which test our resolution, and in which our resolution too often fails, come in the course of daily life: we do indeed need God's guidance, if we are to avoid what the Church calls occasions of sin—situations in which some special weakness of our own may be tested—as a man fighting his way out of alcoholism might be wise to avoid cocktail parties.

The situation that is dangerous to one man need not be so to another. The guidance-away that we need is special to each of us, tailored by the Spirit to each one's weakness. There is no petition in the Lord's Prayer so practically urgent and so continually needed.

In that same first chapter James shifts to the other meaning of ''tempt,'' the meaning it has in modern speech. ''Let no one say when he is tempted 'I am tempted by God,' for God . . . tempts no one. But each person is tempted when he is lured and enticed by his own desire. Desire when it has conceived gives birth to sin; and sin when it is full grown brings forth death.''

Most of the situations that test our moral resolution are of our own contriving. Affections we were quite sure were platonic can in the blink of an eye turn aristotelian, so to speak—(I hope that great philospher will forgive me). The clerk uses the firm's money in the certainty that he can put it back tomorrow, finds that he cannot, and steals larger sums to cover his first small filching. Often enough we haven't a notion of what we are getting into, and suddenly we are in it up to the neck. We live in the confidence that it cannot happen to us. Few of us have never been in the position of the small boy at the party who is quite sure that one more cake will not make him sick: he seldom fails to find the one that does.

When in saying the Our Father we come to Lead us not into temptation, we may not realize that "us" might be the deciding word. The same Christ who told us to ask God not to *lead* us into temptation also gave "Watch and pray lest you *enter into* temptation. For the spirit is willing, but the flesh is weak." By our determination to play with fire we set a problem for anyone who would guide us. Even God. St. Paul says it to the Corinthians (I Cor. 10.12): "Let anyone who thinks he stands take heed lest he fall. No temptation has overtaken you that is not common to man. God is faithful, and he will not let you be tempted beyond your strength,"—thus as we have seen he interprets "Lead us not into temptation." He continues "but with the temptation will also provide the way of escape, that you may be able to endure it," which we may read as his understanding of "Deliver us from evil."

It will be observed that James, who may have been on the Mount to hear the Sermon, and Paul who could hardly have been, have both given their minds to "lead us not into temptation."

BUT DELIVER US FROM EVIL

This is the second of the petitions not in Luke's version. Like the first, it is a way of resaying the one before it from a different angle and casting light in the re-saying. *Lead* us not into temptation is a prayer to be kept from sin. *Deliver* us from evil has the same general idea, but with the more-than-suggestion of a rescue operation—if we do fall into sin, we pray to be helped out of it. In this matter Jesus was wholly realist. He could say to the paralyzed man he healed by the Sheep Gate: "Go, sin no more": but he added: "Lest some worse thing befall you."

The Greek could be read as meaning "Deliver us from the Evil One." In the parable of the Sower (Matthew 13) "the evil one," *ho poneros,* "snatches away what is sown in the heart." In the explanation of the parable, verse 39, Christ translates this as "the devil."

And with the temptings in the desert in his mind, Jesus might very well have meant this here.

One of the modern Christian's difficulties about believing in the devil is that, with our own desires so perverse and so mastering, we wonder what the devil can find to do. My own theory is that he has two main fields of operation—the saints and communities, from small groups up to nations. To follow up communities would take us too far from the Lord's Prayer, which as I must continually remind myself is our topic.

But saints, and those who may fall short of sainthood yet are making a real effort at it, may tempt Satan to tempt them. Judas Iscariot, for instance, was an Apostle: when Christ chose him (after a night of prayer) and he accepted the call, he must have had genuine idealism: it was into his head that Satan put the idea of betraying Jesus. Paul gives us a different example. He warns the married "not to refuse each other, except by agreement and for a time. But then come together again lest Satan tempt you through lack of self-control."

But the Lord's Prayer is not solely for those who strive for virtue, still less is it solely for nations. It is for everybody. And my feeling is that the evil we are to be delivered from covers the whole vast area of evil, suffering as well as sin.

Pause upon the phrase "deliver from." Delivery was an idea rooted deep in the Jewish mind from the time when the Lord "came down to deliver them out of the hand of the Egyptians" (Exodus 3.8). In the New Testament especially, the word stands for delivery from every kind of bondage.

In the Epistle to the Hebrews (2.14) we read that Christ took human nature in order that he might die and thus "destroy him who has the power of death, that is, the devil, and *deliver* all those who through fear of death were subject to life-long bondage."

Paul phrased it to the Colossians (1.13): "He has *delivered* us from the dominion of darkness and transferred us to the dominion of his beloved Son."

Sin is always bondage, always darkness. To the Galatians he wrote that Christ died "to *deliver* us from this present evil age"— in fact from the world as John summarized it—"the lust of the flesh and the lust of the eyes and the pride of life."

We may let St. Paul have the last word here—"The creation itself will be delivered from its bondage to decay and obtain the glorious liberty of the sons of God." That is what the Lord's Prayer is about. That is what the Lord is about.

At the end of the Lord's Prayer, Christians outside the Roman Communion say: "For thine is the kingdom and the power and the glory for ever and ever. Amen."

There seems to be universal agreement that it is not part of the Lord's Prayer as the Lord gave it. But it was a Jewish custom to end prayers with some such words on God's glory, and this one was already given as being said at the end of the Lord's Prayer in the *Didache* before the first century was over.

It echoes a prayer said by David "in the presence of all the assembly" (1 Chronicles 29.11): "Thine, O Lord, is the greatness and the power and the glory and the victory and the majesty . . . thine is the kingdom, O Lord.''

It is a splendid prayer and Catholics now have it in the Canon of the Mass.